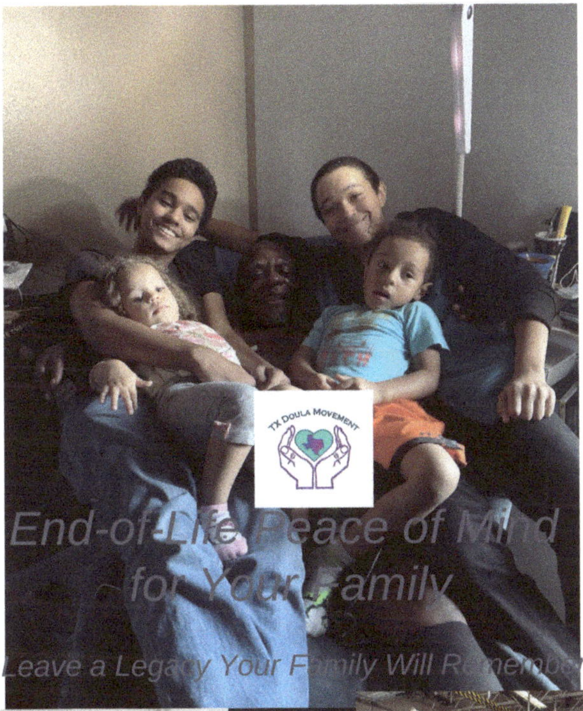

TX DOULA MOVEMENT

End-of-Life Peace of Mind for Your Family

Leave a Legacy Your Family Will Remember

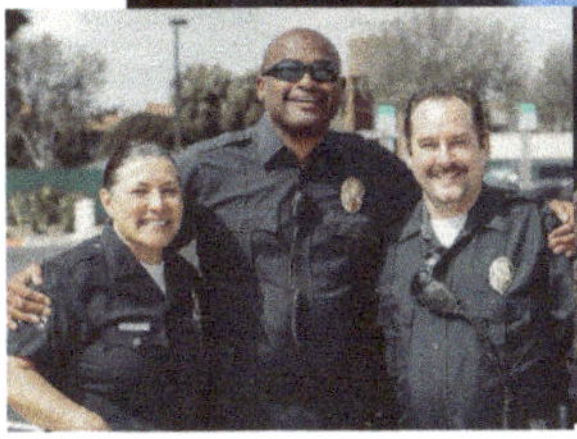

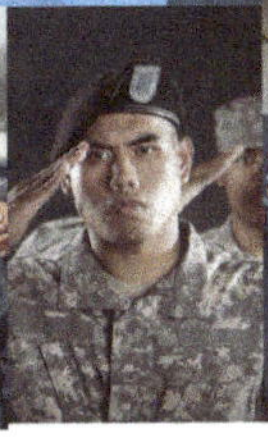

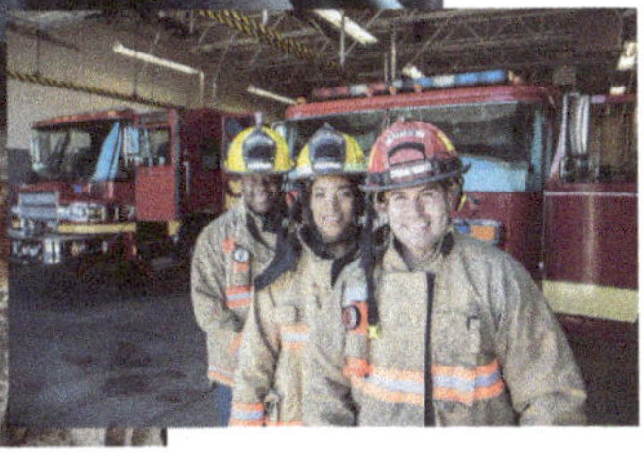

SONJA S. KOENIG / EMMA JANE FRAZIER
WWW.TXDOULAMVMNT.COM

To request permission, contact the author at
doulasupport@txdoulamvmnt.com.

Contact Information:
TX Doula Movement, LLC.
doulasupport@txdoulamvmnt.com
www.txdoulamvmnt.com

Publishers: Sparkling Light Publishers
sparklinglightpublishers@gmail.com
+23409024835120

Purposeful Planning

The church that I attend is called The Purpose Church (located in Schertz, TX.) When the name of our church was changed to The Purpose Church, I thought how odd. However, the more I thought about it and listened to Pastor Landon's sermons, I realized that it wasn't odd. I have a purpose. God has a plan for me.

Jeremiah 29:11 says, "For I know the plans I have for you," declares the LORD, "plans to prosper you and not to harm you, plans to give you hope and a future."

I believe part of the plans God has for me is to share with others the importance of planning for their End-of-life, and how they can be a support to those that are dying and their families.
t

Sonja S. Koenig

Purposeful Planning

A week after I got married, my husband and I completed our paperwork
for our End-of-Life care. You never know when your time is up.
I encourage you to be prepared and plan early. Don't believe the thought that
this is so morbid because it is not. It is love.

You are making plans for your loved ones
so they won't have to go through unnecessary hassles and crisis after you are gone.
It will give them a chance to mourn and not have to look around for paperwork
to complete your affairs. Do it for them. Let them see that part of your purpose
was to get your affairs in order for your family.

Purposeful Planning

How often have you heard about the death of someone's family member? Did you see or hear the families struggle in trying to figure out where their loved one's paperwork was? Did you hear the frustration in their voice because they did not know where the burial insurance or life insurance policy was? Or better yet, you did not know the passwords to bank accounts, who has the mortgage on the house, or if the car is paid for? Those are all good questions.

Once you complete this book, you will eliminate those questions and frustrations. You will also be leaving a legacy for your family by knowing that you wanted your passing to be a little less stressful for them.

Give your family the gift of preparation, because you showed them the importance of planning for your End-of-Life by completing this booklet, they in return will plan for theirs. You have just impacted several generations in your family because you have made your End-of-Life a little more peaceful for your family.

Purposeful Planning

This booklet is to help you plan on purpose. It is a comprehensive checklist that may take you several hours to complete. You will need documents that have been filed away years ago or possibly been forgotten about. This task may be very tedious. It is very important and will benefit you and your loved ones.

We recommend you look over this checklist to see what you will need first. Then gather the paperwork you will need to complete the checklist. You may not be able to locate some of the documents. Do the best you can to complete this checklist. When the missing documents appear, complete the checklist. You may find changes need to be made. That is why it is very important to do an annual review of your affairs.

The time you spend completing this checklist will be beneficial to both you and your family. It is our belief that you will receive personal satisfaction knowing your affairs are in order and you have control in leaving a valuable legacy with your family.

Important Information

This is a list of information/documents you may need to complete this book. If you do not have any of the below documents, do not panic. Gather what you can. Having these documents will make your task so much easier.

Birth Certificate
Social Security Card
Marriage License and/or Divorce Decree
Spouse's Death Certificate
Parent's Death Certificate
Name of ALL Children (biological, adopted, heart adopted, etc.)
- Place of Birth
- Date of Birth
- Address
- Phone #
- Spouse
- Names of their Children (Grand-children)

Military Status (If no military service, then put N/A)
- Date of Entry/Exit
- DD214
- VA Claim #

Law Enforcement Information
Fire Department Information

Important Information

Education Information (Name of institution, year graduated and degree)
- High School
- Trade School
- College
- University

Occupation
- Name of Employer
- Date Started/Ended
- Position

Important Contacts
- Religious Affiliation
- Legal Representation
- CPA/Tax Preparer

Insurance Documents
- Life Insurance Policy
- Funeral Benefits
- Annuity
- Retirement

Banking Documents

Investment Information
- Stocks
- Mutual Funds
- Other: _______________________

End-of-Life Documents
- Medical Power of Attorney
- Directive to Physician
- Out-of-Hospital Do-Not-Resuscitate
- Medical Order for Scope of Treatment
- Organ Donation
- Last Will and Testament
- Living Trust/Irrevocable Trust

Assets & Liabilities
- Mortgage Information
- Property Notes (rental, land, etc.)
- Vehicle Note Holder (car, truck, motorcycle, etc.)

Online Presence (email addresses, passwords, website, etc.)

Important Dates

Funeral Home Contact

IT'S OKAY, YOU ARE GOING TO DIE

We all have experienced loss, in some way or another. You have lost your keys, wallet, job, home, pet, loved one, etc. Loss is inevitable. Death is inevitable. We will all go through the loss of something or the death of someone. How do you handle death? Where is God when you lose someone precious to you? Will you ever be whole again? How can you go on? If you've ever lost a loved one, you're probably asking these questions.

Take this time to think about death. You can't be there for someone who is dying if you have not dealt with your own thoughts on your mortality. What are your own personal views concerning death, dying, and the afterlife? Have you taken the time to write your obituary or eulogy? At the end of this booklet, you will find a guide to help you write your obituary and eulogy. This will help you think about your life and how you want to be remembered. You will have control over what is said about you and how it is said.

Embrace the process of preparing yourself for your death and having your wishes met.

In this section, you will add
important information
about yourself, your family,
and your fur babies.

ALL ABOUT
YOU!

*Essential Information You May Need
for Your End-of-Life Planning*

■ Full Legal Name: _______________________________________

■ Date of Birth: _______________ Place of Birth: _______________

■ Location of Birth Certificate: _______________________________

■ Social Security Number: _______________________________

■ Legal Residence: _______________________________

■ Address: _______________________________________

■ Name of Spouse: _______________________________

■ Date of Marriage: _______________________________

■ Date of Divorce: _______________________________

■ Date of Death: _______________________________

■ Place of Death: _______________________________

SPOUSES
GALORE!

Essential Information You May Need
for Your End-of-Life Planning

You may have had more than one spouse. Use this
space to list any additional spouses you have had. If
there are no additional spouses mark N/A in the lines.

Name of Spouse: _______________________________________

Date of Marriage: ______________________________________

Date of Divorce: _______________________________________

Date of Death: ____

Place of Death: ____

Name of Spouse: _______________________________________

Date of Marriage:_______________________________________

Date of Divorce: _______________________________________

Date of Death: ____

Place of Death: ____

PARENTS ARE IMPORTANT

*Essential Information You May Need
for Your End-of-Life Planning*

Mother's Name: ____

Address: ____

Date of Birth: ____

Place of Birth: ____

Date of Death: ____

Place of Death   : ____

Father's Name: ____

Address :   ____

Date of Birth : ____

Place of Birth: ____

Date of Death: ____

Place of Death: ____

DON'T FORGET
CHILDREN

*Essential Information You May Need
for Your End-of-Life Planning*

Name of Child1: _______________________________________

Date of Birth: _______________________________________

Place of Birth: _______________________________________

Address: _______________________________________

Child's Spouse: _______________________________________

Phone #: _______________________________________

Name of Child2: _______________________________________

Date of Birth: _______________________________________

Place of Birth: _______________________________________

Address: _______________________________________

Phone #: _______________________________________

Child's Spouse: _______________________________________

DON'T FORGET
CHILDREN

*Essential Information You May Need
for Your End-of-Life Planning*

- Name of Child3: _______________________________________

- Date of Birth   : _______________________________________

- Place of Birth: _______________________________________

- Address: _______________________________________

- Phone #: _______________________________________

- Child's Spouse   : _______________________________________

- Name of Child4 : _______________________________________

- Date of Birth   : _______________________________________

- Place of Birth: _______________________________________

- Address: _______________________________________

- Phone #: _______________________________________

- Child's Spouse: _______________________________________

DON'T FORGET
CHILDREN

*Essential Information You May Need
for Your End-of-Life Planning*

- Name of Child5: _______________________________________
- Date of Birth: _______________________________________
- Place of Birth: _______________________________________
- Address : _______________________________________
- Phone #: _______________________________________
- Child's Spouse: _______________________________________
- Name of Child6: _______________________________________
- Date of Birth: _______________________________________
- Place of Birth: _______________________________________
- Address: _______________________________________
- Phone #: _______________________________________
- Child's Spouse: _______________________________________

DON'T FORGET
CHILDREN
*Essential Information You May Need
for Your End-of-Life Planning*

Name of Child7: ____

Date of Birth: ____

Place of Birth: ____

Address: ____

Phone #: ____

Child's Spouse: ____

Name of Child8: ____

Date of Birth: ____

Place of Birth: ____

Address: ____

Phone #: ____

Child's Spouse: ____

DON'T FORGET
FUR BABY

You may or may not have a fur baby. If you do, it is important that you leave detailed information about your fur baby.

Type of Pet: ___________________________________

Name of Pet: ___________________________________

Pets DOB/Age: ___________________________________

Hlth/Diet Needs: ___________________________________

Veterinarian: ___________________________________

Veterinarian Phone #: ___________________________________

Pet Insurance #: ___________________________________

Favorite Activities/Treats/Toys: ___________________________
____

If service/emotional support, where are papers located:
____

Grooming Tips:___________________________________

Microchip #: ___________________________________

New Guardian: ___________________________________

Phone #: ___________________________________

Additional Information: ___________________________
____

DON'T FORGET
FUR BABY

You may or may not have a fur baby. If you do, it is important that you leave detailed information about your fur baby.

■ Type of Pet: _______________________________________

■ Name of Pet: _______________________________________

■ Pets DOB/Age: ______________________________ ______

■ Hlth/Diet Needs: ____________________________________

■ Veterinarian: _______________________________________

■ Veterinarian Phone #: _______________________________

■ Pet Insurance #: ____________________________________

■ Favorite Activities/Treats/Toys: _______________________
____

■ If service/emotional support, where are papers located:
____

■ Grooming Tips:______________________________________

■ Microchip #: _______________________________________

■ New Guardian: ______________________________________

■ Phone #: ____

■ Additional Information: _______________________________
____

In the next section, you will add important information about your service in the military, law enforcement, or fire department.

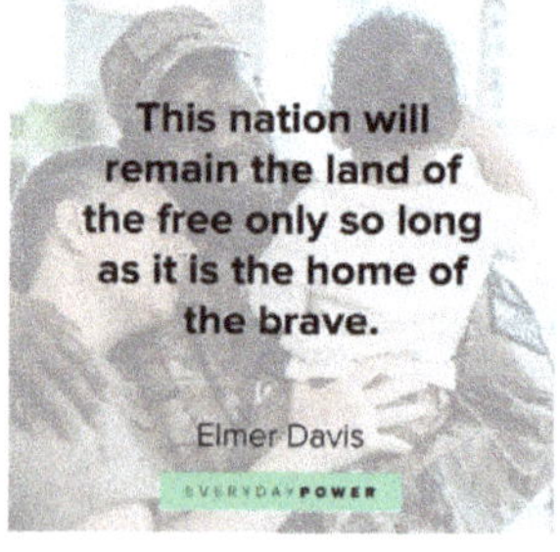

THANK YOU FOR
YOUR SERVICE

Essential Information You May Need
for Your End-of-Life Planning

Military Branch   : ____

Date of Entry : ____

Date of Discharge: _______________________________________

Location of DD214: _______________________________________

VA Claim #:____
(Survivors should contact VA or 1-800-827-1000 to report death and discontinue benefits.)

High School:____

Year Graduated:____

College:____

Year Graduated:____

Degree:____

College:____

Year Graduated:____

Degree:____

THANK YOU FOR
YOUR SERVICE

*Essential Information You May Need for
Your End-of-Life Planning*

■ Law Enforcement Agency : _______________________________

■ Date of Entry: _______________________________________

■ Date of Discharge: ___________________________________

■ Rank/Badge#: ____

■ Next of Kin:____

■ Relationship: ___________________________ Phone#: ______________

■ Address:_______________________________ ___________________________

■ Combination to Gun Safe: _____________________________

■ Gun Safe Key Location: _______________________________

■ Union Name:____

■ Union Rep Full Name:_________________________________

■ Phone # of Rep:______________________________________

■ Status of Law Enforcement Relationship

■ Active Duty:___________   ■ Retired:___________________

■ Reserved:___________   ■ Other:___________________

THANK YOU FOR
YOUR SERVICE

Essential Information You May Need
for Your End-of-Life Planning

Fire Department Agency   : _______________________________________

Date of Entry: _______________________________________

Date of Discharge: _______________________________________

Rank/Badge#: _______________________________________

Next of Kin:_______________________________________

Relationship: ____________________________ Phone #: ________________

Address: ____

Combination to Locker: ____________________________________

Locker Key Location: ______________________________________

Union Name:______________________________________

Union Rep Full Name:______________________________________

Phone # of Rep:______________________________________

Status of Fire Department Relationship

Active Duty:____________   Retired:____________________

Reserved:____________   Other:____________________

In the next section, you will
add important information
about your employment
and retirement   .

MY
OCCUPATION
Essential Information You May
Need for Your End-of-Life Planning

Name of Employer: ___________________________________

Date of Entered: ___________ ___________________________

Date of Exit: _______________________________________

Position: ____

Name of Employer: ___________________________________

Date of Entered: _____________________________________

Date of Exit: _______________________________________

Position: ____

Name of Employer: ___________________________________

Date of Entered: _____________________________________

Date of Exit: _______________________________________

Position: ____

MY
OCCUPATION

*Essential Information You May
Need for Your End-of-Life Planning*

Name of Employer: _______________________________________

Date of Entered: ____

Date of Exit: ____

Position: ____

Name of Employer: _______________________________________

Date of Entered: ____

Date of Exit: ____

Position: ____

Name of Employer: _______________________________________

Date of Entered: ____

Date of Exit: ____

Position: ____

MY
OCCUPATION

*Essential Information You May Need
for Your End-of-Life Planning*

- Name of Employer: _______________________________________

- Date of Entered: _______________________________________

- Date of Exit: _______________________________________

- Position: _______________________________________

- Name of Employer: _______________________________________

- Date of Entered: _______________________________________

- Date of Exit: _______________________________________

- Position: _______________________________________

- Name of Employer: _______________________________________

- Date of Entered: _______________________________________

- Date of Exit: _______________________________________

- Position: _______________________________________

READY FOR
RETIREMENT

*Essential Paperwork to Have
for Your End-of-Life Planning*

Insurance Documents: Policy Holders/Phone Number

Annuity: _______________________________________

Phone #: _______________________________________

Address: _______________________________________

____

Annuity:

____

Phone #: _______________________________________

Address: _______________________________________

____

Retirement: _______________________________________

Phone #: _______________________________________

Address: _______________________________________

____

In the next section, you will
add important contacts.
Make sure you include
addresses, phone numbers,
and your relationship to the
person.

The most important
people in my life are the
ones who have more
faith in me than I do
myself. And for that, I
am truly blessed.

PictureQuotes.com

IMPORTANT
CONTACTS

*Essential Information You May Need
for Your End-of-Life Planning*

Religious Affiliation:____________________________________

Name of Church: ______________________________________

Pastor: ____

Phone #: ____

Address: ____

Important Contacts: ___________________________________

Attorney: ____

Phone #: ____

Banker: ____

Phone #: ____

CPA/Tax Preparer: ____________________________________

Phone #: ____

IMPORTANT
CONTACTS

*Essential Information You May Need
for Your End-of-Life Planning*

Name:____

Address: ____

Phone #: ____

Relationship #: ____

Name:____

Address: ____

Phone #: ____

Relationship #: ____

Name:____

Address: ____

Phone #: ____

Relationship #: ____

IMPORTANT
CONTACTS

*Essential Information You May Need
for Your End-of-Life Planning*

Name:____

Address: ____

Phone #: ____

Relationship #: ____

Name:____

Address: ____

Phone #: ____

Relationship #: ____

Name:____

Address: ____

Phone #: ____

Relationship #: ____

IMPORTANT
CONTACTS

*Essential Information You May Need for
Your End-of-Life Planning*

Name :____

Address: ____

Phone #: ____

Relationship #: ____

Name:____

Address: ____

Phone #: ____

Relationship #: ____

Name:____

Address: ____

Phone #: ____

Relationship #: ____

In the next section, you will add important documents

INSURANCE
DOCUMENTS
Essential Paperwork You May Need
for Your End-of-Life Planning

▪ Insurance Documents: Policy Holders/Phone Number

▪ Burial: ____

▪ Phone #: ____

▪ Address: ____

____

▪ Life: ____

▪ Phone #: ____

▪ Address: ____

____

▪ Life: ____

▪ Phone #: ____

▪ Address: ____

____

BANKING
INFORMATION

*Essential Paperwork to Have for Your
End-of-Life Planning*

Banking Documents: _______________________________________

Account #: ____

Type: ____

Location: ____

Phone #: ____

Address: ____

____

Banking Documents: _______________________________________

Account #: ____

Type: ____

Location: ____

Phone #: ____

Address:____

____

BANKING
INFORMATION

*Essential Paperwork to Have for Your
End-of-Life Planning*

Banking Documents: ______________________________ ______

Account #: ____

Type: ____

Location: ____

Phone #: ____

Address: ____

____

Banking Documents: _____________________________________

Account #: ____

Type: ____

Location: ____

Phone #: ____

Address: ____

____

MY
INVESTMENTS

*Essential Paperwork to Have for Your
End-of-Life Planning*

☐ Investment Information: (Stocks, Mutual Funds, etc.)

☐ Account #: ____

☐ Type: ____

☐ Company: ____

☐ Phone #: ____

☐ Address: ____

____

☐ Investment Information: (Stocks, Mutual Funds, etc.)

☐ Account: ____

☐ Type: ____

☐ Company: ____

☐ Phone #: ____

☐ Address: ____

____

MY
INVESTMENTS

*Essential Paperwork to Have for Your
End-of-Life Planning*

Investment Information: (Stocks, Mutual Funds, etc.)

Account #: _______________________________________

Type: ____

Company: ____

Phone #: ____

Address: ____

____

Investment Information: (Stocks, Mutual Funds, etc.)

Account #: _______________________________________

Type: ____

Company: ____

Phone #: ____

Address: ____

____

ASSETS & LIABILITIES

Essential End-of-Life Documents
List Location of Documents

■ Property Address: _______________________________

____

■ Mortgage Amount: _______________________________

■ Mortgage Holder: _______________________________

■ Phone #: _______________________________________

■ Date Sold/Sale Price: ___________________ /____________

■ Property Address:_______________________________

■ Mortgage Amount: _______________________________

■ Mortgage Holder: _______________________________

■ Phone #: _______________________________________

■ Date Sold/Sale Price: ___________________ /____________

ASSETS & LIABILITIES

Essential End-of-Life Documents
List Location of Documents

- Property Address:____

  ____

- Mortgage Amount: ____

- Mortgage Holder: ____

- Phone #: ____

- Date Sold/Sale Price: ___________________ /___________________

- Vehicle Make/Model/Year: _________________________________

- Color____

- VIN: ____

- Lien Holder: ____

- Phone #: ____

- Date Purchase: ____

- Location of vehicle: _______________________________________

In the next section, you will add your end-of-life documents and care plan. Put copies of the documents in this section.

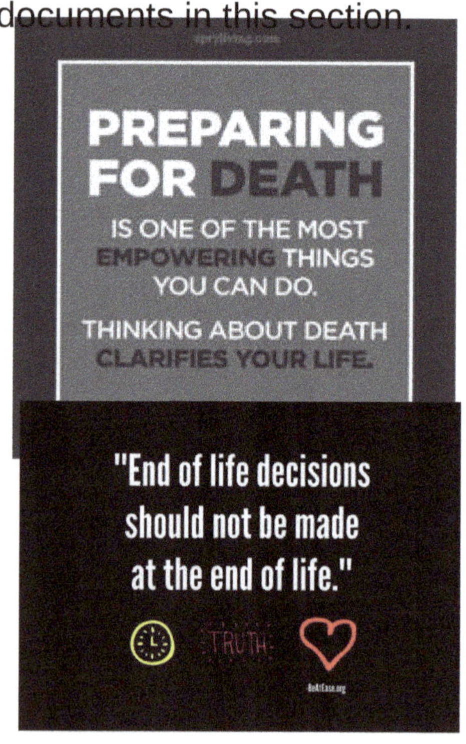

END-OF-LIFE
DECISIONS

Essential End-of-Life Documents
List Location of Documents

- MedicalPower of Attorney: _______________________________

- Name of Proxy1: _______________________________________

- Phone #: ____

- Name of Proxy2: _______________________________________

- Phone #: ____

- Living Will: ____

- Out-of-Hospital-Do Not Resuscitate:_______________________

- Medical Order for Scope of Treatment: ____________________

- Organ Donation: ____

- Last Will & Testament: ___________________________________

- Trust: ____

In the next section, you will add
your one-line life. Not everyone
can remember their password.
Your family definitely will not
know yours unless you record
them here.

MY ONLINE
LIFE

Important Digital Information
(Email Addresses, Passwords, Websites, Etc.)

Name: ____

Website: ____

Email Address: ____

Password: ____

Name: ____

Website: ____

Email Address: ____

Password: ____

Name: ____

Website: ____

Email Address: ____

Password: ____

MY ONLINE
LIFE

Important Digital Information
(Email Addresses, Passwords, Websites, Etc.)

Name: ____

Website: ____

Email Address: ___________________________________

Password: ____

Name: ____

Website: ____

Email Address: ___________________________________

Password: ____

Name: ____

Website: ____

Email Address: ___________________________________

Password: ____

MY ONLINE
LIFE

Important Digital Information
(Email Addresses, Passwords, Websites, Etc.)

Name: ____

Website: ____

Email Address: _______________________________________

Password: ____

Name: ____

Website: ____

Email Address: _______________________________________

Password: ____

Name: ____

Website: ____

Email Address: _______________________________________

Password: ____

MY ONLINE
LIFE

*Important Digital Information
(Email Addresses, Passwords, Websites, Etc.)*

Name: ____

Website: ____

Email Address: ____

Password: ____

Name: ____

Website: ____

Email Address: ____

Password: ____

Name: ____

Website: ____

Email Address: ____

Password: ____

In the next section, you will add important dates. We all have important dates in our life. Do you remember all of yours?

DATES TO REMEMBER

Important Dates & Information
(Birthdates, Anniversaries, Deaths)

■ Name: ____

■ DOB: ____

■ DOD: ____

■ Anniversary: _________________________________

■ Information:__________________________________

____

____

■ Name: ____

■ DOB: ____

■ DOD: ____

■ Anniversary: _________________________________

■ Information: _________________________________

____

____

DATES TO REMEMBER

Important Dates & Information
(Birthdates, Anniversaries, Deaths)

Name: _______________________________________

DOB: _______________________________________

DOD: _______________________________________

Anniversary: _______________________________________

Information: _______________________________________

____

Name: _______________________________________

DOB: _______________________________________

DOD: _______________________________________

Anniversary: _______________________________________

Information: _______________________________________

____

DATES TO
REMEMBER
Important Dates & Information
(Birthdates, Anniversaries, Deaths)

Name: ____

DOB: ____

DOD: ____

Anniversary: ____

Information:____

____

____

Name: ____

DOB: ____

DOD: ____

Anniversary: ____

Information: ____

____

____

In the next section, you will make
your funeral arrangements, and
write your obituary and eulogy.
Make sure you include pictures
that you want on your program
and obituary.

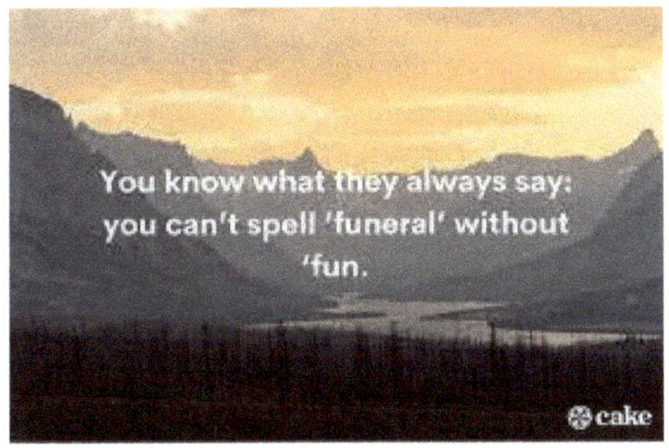

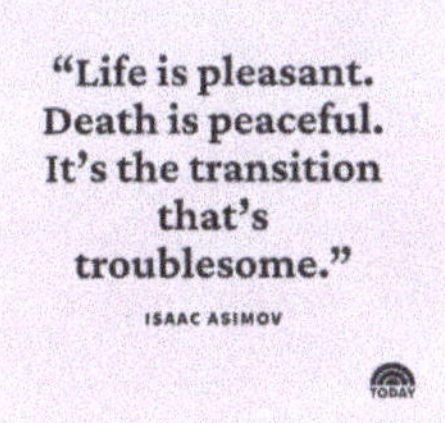

FUNERAL ARRANGEMENTS

Why Prearrange Your Funeral?

How many times have you prearranged a wedding, vacation, birth of a child, etc? Why not prearrange your funeral, or homegoing (as I like to call it)? Why do we wait until someone has passed to make funeral arrangements? Making funeral arrangements after you have passed will not be an easy task for your family. Timeframes are short, the added burden of grief makes it difficult to deal with planning, and financial concerns may arise among your family members. Give your family a gift and make arrangements for them. This section will help you in your pre-planning.

What will planning do for your family?
- Ease their burden
- Assume the financial responsibility for your funeral
- Your family will have the benefit of a meaningful funeral
- Your final wishes will be followed
- Be self-reliant and have your affairs in order at the end

FUNERAL ARRANGEMENTS

Why Prearrange Your Funeral?

Some tips on cutting the cost of your funeral:
1. Buy your casket from COSTCO, SAM'S, Amazon, or a Casket Company cheaper and have it shipped to the funeral home. You do not have to purchase your casket from the funeral home.
2. Have a home wake and a home funeral, and then have the body moved to a funeral home for body disposal.
3. You do not have to be embalmed (check with your state law and funeral home policies).
4. Plan your own program and have it printed yourself.
5. Have your body donated to science. After they have finished with your body, they will cremate it for free and give your family the ashes.
6. Order your flower arrangements locally instead of from the funeral home.
7. Have a graveside funeral service.

FUNERAL ARRANGEMENTS

Funeral Arrangment Choices

- ☐ Disposition of Remains (Body Disposal):

- ☐ Traditional Burial
- ☐ Cremation

- ☐ Green Burial
- ☐ Other: _______________________

- ☐ Burial Vault
- ☐ Below Ground

- ☐ Cremation Urn
- ☐ Above Ground

- ☐ Casket
- ☐ Coffin

- ☐ Clergy/Officiant: _______________________________________

- ☐ Musician/Organist: _____________________________________

- ☐ Eulogy Reader: ____

- ☐ Scripture Reader: _______________________________________

- ☐ Soloist: ____

- ☐ Song: ____

FUNERAL
ARRANGEMENTS
Funeral Arrangment Choices

☐ Pallbearer:_______________________________________

☐ _______________________________________

☐ _______________________________________

☐ _______________________________________

☐ _______________________________________

☐ _______________________________________

☐ _______________________________________

☐ Poem Reader: _______________________________________

☐ Soloist: _______________________________________

☐ Closing Remarks: _______________________________________

☐ Reception: _______________________________________

ADDITIONAL FUNERAL WISHES

This is the space for you to write additional funeral wishes, such as food at your repass/reception.

____

____

____

____

____

____

____

____

____

____

____

____

____

____

____

____

MY
OBITUARY

Write Your Obituary
(Take this time to write what you want to be said about you.)

A long-standing custom is for a funeral director or newspaper reporter to compile information on the deceased and write the obituary. By writing your own obituary, you choose the focus and the information that will be shared. Here are some tips:

1. **Write in the third-person perspective.** It might seem obvious to some, but it's important to follow the form in this way. Feel free to spice up the narrative with some self-aware humor (e.g. "Sarah was a modest woman; a fact that she pointed out to everyone she met") but stay within the structure.

2. **Do not be concerned about tradition.** Obituaries often hit up the main thrust of the deceased's life—where they were born, where they went to school, whom they married, and occupation, etc. You should feel free to talk about

MY
OBITUARY
Write Your Obituary

those subjects, if you like, but it is not mandatory.
Write about what's been most important to you. Sum
up those experiences, anecdotes, and life-changing
moments in a succinct summary. One person might
write, "After spending two years in a monastery in
Tibet, Samantha became a devout student of
Buddhism," while another might simply say, "Paul's
three children were the most important part of his
life." Whatever matters most to you should be
emphasized.

3. **Trim it down.** Your life is important, especially to
you. There's going to be a lot that you think is essential
reading. Remember, you are trying to impart the
essence of your life, not grind out every detail of it.
Stick to a couple of anecdotes, some choice life events,
dates, a few details, and/or personality traits. Do not
write a novel.

MY
OBITUARY
Write Your Obituary

4. **Update it regularly, especially after major life events.** If you write your obituary before you get married or have children, your family may not want to use it. Keep it relevant. Feel free to keep old drafts to show you what your life and your sense of self were like.

5. **Skip the secrets and gossip.** If there are some things you do not want to tell your family or friends while you are alive, do not put that information in your obituary. An obituary is a public community report. Spilling a secret in that manner can place more shock and pain on an already grieving loved one. Instead, write personal letters disclosing the private information, with instructions on how close or public you'd like it to remain. Avoid being cruel or insulting to family or friends in your obituary. It might seem funny when you write it, but these will be your last words about your loved ones. They will be public.

MY
OBITUARY
Write Your Obituary

6. **Make notes for your family.** Unless you are writing your obituary in the last stages of a long illness, you are not aware of how or when you are going to die. You do not know everything that will happen to you between writing the draft and the end of your life. You can make things easier on your family by leaving notes underneath your obituary for possible scenarios (e.g. "If I am murdered or killed in a car accident, please leave out the cause of death. If I die of an illness, you may mention it briefly. If I slip and die in the shower with a doughnut in my hand, just say, 'He passed peacefully in his sleep.'")

Now that you have given this guide for writing your obituary, sit down and write it. Don't put it off or let someone else write it. You are the guide on what will be said about you.

MY
OBITUARY
Write Your Obituary

Find a recent photo of yourself to add to your obituary. You might want to include a photo of a younger one along with a current photo of yourself. This will help the friends of your youth recognize you.

If you want your obituary in the local paper, check the cost and decide when you want it posted, right after your death or days before your funeral service. Make a note of this information and keep it handy for your family. You might want to set some money aside for them to pay for the posting.

WRITE YOUR OBITUARY

This is the space for you to write your obituary.

This is the space for you to write your obituary.

MY
EULOGY
Write Your Eulogy

Writing your eulogy can be a little difficult, especially if you have never written a eulogy. Who is more qualified to write your eulogy than you? There are several different types of eulogies you can write. The easiest eulogy to write is a chronological eulogy. Well then, let's get started.

Let us begin with an outline.

Sit in a comfortable chair with a cup of tea (I'm not a coffee drinker) and just imagine God will give you the gift of life until you are 100 and then you pass away. Now picture what you have done during your 10 decades of life. Where you lived, whom you loved, how you acted. This is your life as you hope to have lived it. Jot down some memories of yourself in answer to the following questions.

MY
EULOGY

Write Your Eulogy

- **Where did you live?** Did you stay in the town in which you were born? Did you live in another country? Did you move every few years? Where did you retire?
- **What were your hobbies?** What did you enjoy doing in your 20's and 30's? What did you enjoy doing with your family? What kept you busy in retirement?
- **What kind of relationships did you have?** Did you get married? How many children did you have? Did you have many close friends?
- **Where did you go to school?** What did you study?
- **What was your occupation?** How long were you employed? Did you change careers often?

MY
EULOGY
Write Your Eulogy

- **Awards.** Did you win any awards or accomplish any noteworthy feats?
- **What was most memorable about you?** Did you have a sense of humor? Were you a good cook? Did you have a love for adventure and a passion for the outdoors? Did you have unshakable faith?
- **What did people admire about you most?** Did you have unwavering loyalty to your friends? Did you have integrity and good work ethics? Did you have much love for your family? Did you have patience and good leadership?
- **What will people miss most about you?** Did you give creative homemade gifts every Christmas? Were you a good listener? Did you write handwritten letters to your friends? Did you turn every mishap into something to laugh about?

MY EULOGY

Write Your Eulogy

The second thing you want to do is write your eulogy.

Now you're going to take all of the ideas you just wrote down and integrate them into a finished project. This format is easy to follow and will give you the outcome you need to complete your eulogy:

1. Birth and childhood. Keep this section brief.
2. College and career. Where did you go to school? What did you major in? What jobs did you have? Include any accomplishments and awards you won.
3. Family and relationships.
4. Your hobbies and interests
5. The qualities and characteristics that set you apart and made you memorable.
6. What people will miss about you?

MY
EULOGY
Write Your Eulogy

Here's your assignment:

Take all the information you have written and **write your own eulogy.** Confront your mortality and really give some thought about how you want to be remembered. Take your time and be as creative as you want.

You have taken control over what will be read about you and what you want people to know about you. Now decide the person you want to read your eulogy for you. Better yet, make a video and read it yourself and have someone play it for everyone at your funeral.

WRITE YOUR EULOGY

This is the space for you to write your eulogy.

WRITE YOUR EULOGY

This is the space for you to
write your eulogy.

ADDITIONAL NOTES

*(More information you want your family to know,
  such as phone numbers and addresses of friends.)*

ADDITIONAL NOTES

*(More information you want your
family to know.)*

SAMPLE
FUNERAL
PROGRAM

One of the many questions we have received from families that are putting together their loved ones' funeral/memorial program is, "How do I put a program together?" We have put together a sample program for you. You can use this as a format or create your own. Putting together a program is really not as hard as you think it is. It can be as simple or as elegant as you would like.

This sample is not set in stone. Be creative. You can add a page or two of pictures of your loved one and others. This gives people a chance to learn a little bit about the kind of person your loved one was. Your program can be as short or as long as you would like. Remember, your program will represent them, not you.

FUNERAL ③ CUSTOMS
SUGGESTED ORDER OFSERVICE
FOR LAW ENFORCEMENT

Below information is from: https://www.funeralwise.com/funeral-customs/police/

Police Funeral Customs: Where to Start

The starting point for planning an officer's memorial service is the final wishes of the officer if they are known. Law enforcement departments that plan ahead for these occasions are wise to ask each officer to write down exactly what is desired at a memorial. These directives can include the designated department representative (e.g., a close friend in the department), choice of music, pallbearers, clergy, interment, and any other details the officer cares to designate.

With the officer's directives taken into consideration, the family must be consulted. Their wishes outweigh the traditions of the department. It is vital that all options for honoring the fallen officer be presented to the survivors. They need to know not only what should be done (according to tradition), or what has always been done, but also what can be done to memorialize their loved one. It would be a sad situation for the family to learn, after the service, that they could have had the last radio call, but it wasn't part of the department's tradition.

The family can select only those elements of the service they wish to have included. For example, tradition might call for a three-volley salute to be offered at the cemetery; the family may decline because the sound of gunfire would be too traumatic. A "21 Bells" ceremony can be substituted. Again, survivors should understand the options presented but not be pressured into including any tradition.

FUNERAL CUSTOMS
SUGGESTED ORDER OF SERVICE
FOR LAW ENFORCEMENT

Below information is from: https://www.funeralwise.com/funeral-customs/police/

The following suggested order of events would be appropriate for a formal, full-honors funeral.

First, the honor guard designee escorts the family to the staging area, meeting up with the casket. The chief is advised to start the ceremony. At this point, the honor guard (casket detail, pallbearers) performs its duties. They accompany the casket to its place of honor, and the Color Guard presents the colors.

After this ceremony, the funeral service itself begins. Following is an example of the order of events for a religious service:

1. Invocation
2. Prayer
3. Opening remarks/greetings
4. Special music
5. Scripture reading/clergy remarks
6. Speakers
   a. Mayor
   b. Local elected officials from the district
   c. State or Federal officials
   d. Family representative(s)
   e. Union representative
   f. Department representative's friends
7. Eulogy – Chief, dignitaries, and/or family
8. Special music
9. Presentations
10. Closing remarks/prayer

FUNERAL CUSTOMS
SUGGESTED ORDER OF SERVICE
FOR LAW ENFORCEMENT

Below information is from: https://www.funeralwise.com/funeral-customs/police/

11. 21 Bells ceremony (also may be performed at the cemetery)
12. Bagpipes play (Amazing Grace, for example)
13. Final Radio Call ceremony (also may be performed at the cemetery)
14. Color Guard retires the colors
15. Bagpipes play as the Pallbearers remove the casket
16. Dismissal instructions

The honor guard's duties continue during the procession to the cemetery and the interment, with each department following its own procedures. The procession for a Line Of Duty Death (LODD) may include hundreds of cars, and both traffic and parking control are necessary. At the interment, honors may include Last Radio Call, three-volley salute (or 21 bells), flyover, flag folding, playing of Taps, bagpipes, and a dove release.

Police Funeral Customs: Venue
A line of duty death is a tragedy that brings officers, dignitaries, and mourners from surrounding cities, states, and (sometimes) even nations. The venue for the funeral should be large enough to accommodate several thousand mourners and have a parking lot where the procession to the cemetery can be staged. Options can include a school auditorium, a civic auditorium, or a large church.

FUNERAL CUSTOMS
SUGGESTED ORDER OF SERVICE FOR FIREFIGHTERS

Below information is from: https://www.funeralwise.com/funeral-customs/firefighter-types/

Formal Firefighter Funeral with Full Honors
A funeral for a line-of-duty death generally presents the family with many options and traditions for honoring their loved one (Funeral Procedures for Firefighters, National Volunteer Fire Council, Second Edition):

- The use of apparatus
- Pallbearers
- A color guard (optional)
- A funeral detail composed of fire personnel in Class A uniforms
- Badge shrouds
- Bagpipers
- A bell service ("Last Alarm" or "Last Call")
- A bugler
- Crossed ladders at the entrance to the cemetery
- A fire engine caisson
- An honor guard
- Station/vehicle bunting

We can't overemphasize the importance of both determining and respecting the family's wishes in regard to the firefighter funeral service. The Montgomery, NY, Fire Department offers the following **questions to discuss with the family** regarding the wake and funeral for a line-of-duty death:

- Do they want an honor guard at the wake?
- Do they need pallbearers? Who? How many?
- Will there be a church service? If so, where and what time?
- What cemetery will be used for burial?

FUNERAL CUSTOMS
SUGGESTED ORDER OF SERVICE
FOR FIREFIGHTERS

Below information is from: https://www.funeralwise.com/funeral-customs/firefighter-types/

- Do they need to use the firehouse or pavilion for refreshments after the wake or funeral?
- Will there be a procession to the place of interment, and what route will it take?
- Will the apparatus be in the procession and/or used for carrying the casket, flowers, etc.?
- Do they want firefighters to escort the hearse (coffin) in the procession or upon entering the cemetery?
- Do they want bagpipes? Where will they play? Church, procession, cemetery?
- Do they want a "Last Call" and if so, where? Firehouse, cemetery?

The National Volunteer Fire Council suggests these **additional topics** to consider, depending on department procedures:

- Procession route, which may include a drive or walk by the deceased's fire station or home, or other special considerations
- Providing a static display of apparatus if requested and appropriate on the procession route
- Providing crossed ladders or aerial equipment if requested and appropriate at the cemetery entrance

Other topics to discuss would be whether there will be burial or cremation; whether they need help with housing for out-of-town relatives, child care, transportation, or a post-service luncheon; whom they would like to deliver the eulogy; whether they want to designate a cause or charity in lieu of flowers; and other routine questions asked of any family suffering a loss.

FUNERAL CUSTOMS
SUGGESTED ORDER OF SERVICE
FOR FIREFIGHTERS

Below information is from: https://www.funeralwise.com/funeral-customs/firefighter-types/

Semi-Formal Firefighter Funeral with Honors

In the case of an off-duty death of an active department member or affiliate member, the following honors may be given:
- Pallbearers
- Color guard (optional)
- A funeral detail composed of fire personnel in Class A uniforms
- Badge shrouds
- A bell service
- An honor guard
- Station/vehicle bunting

Non-Formal Firefighter Funeral with Honors

If the deceased was a non-firefighting, affiliated, or retired department member or the immediate family of a firefighter, non-formal honors may be given:
- A funeral detail of fire personnel in Class A uniforms
- Badge shrouds
- A bell service
- An honor guard
- Station bunting

Again, these options are dependent on the wishes of the deceased, the preferences of the family, and the resources of the affected fire department. The department should be absolutely certain of its ability to provide a particular tradition or honor before it offers it to the family. For example, if the family wants a color guard, but the department is in a small community and doesn't have its own color guard, it must confirm the availability of a color guard through another department or the American Legion or VFW before promising one for the funeral.

FUNERAL CUSTOMS
SUGGESTED ORDER OF SERVICE
FOR FIREFIGHTERS

Below information is from: https://www.funeralwise.com/funeral-customs/firefighter-types/

Sample Order of Events

For a formal, full-honors funeral (from the Utah State Fire Chiefs Association Firefighter Line-of-Duty Death Guidelines, 2006).

1. Invocation
2. Prayer
3. Opening remarks/greetings
4. Special music
5. Scripture reading/clergy remarks
6. Speakers
    a. Mayor
    b. Local elected officials from the district
    c. State or Federal officials
    d. Family representative(s)
    e. Union representative
    f. Department representative's friends
7. Eulogy – Chief
8. Special music
9. Presentations
10. Closing remarks/prayer
11. Last Alarm ceremony
12. Bagpipes
13. Dismissal instructions

PICTURES
YOU CHOOSE THE PICTURES YOU WANT DISPLAYED.

Don't let someone post a picture you don't want displayed. Tape a copy of the pictures you want to be shown at your service on the next couple of pages. If you don't choose someone might post a picture you didn't want others to see.

PICTURES

YOU CHOOSE THE PICTURES YOU WANT DISPLAYED.

Don't let someone post a picture you don't want displayed. Tape a copy of the pictures you want to be shown at your service on the next couple of pages. If you don't choose someone might post a picture you didn't want others to see.

PICTURES

YOU CHOOSE THE PICTURES YOU WANT DISPLAYED.

Don't let someone post a picture you don't want displayed. Tape a copy of the pictures you want to be shown at your service on the next couple of pages. If you don't choose someone might post a picture you didn't want others to see.

WAY
TO GO!!

You have left your last gift.

Leaving one of the best gifts you can give.

You should feel excited about the last gift you are able to leave your family. This gift of leaving all your important information for your family will make their time of mourning and grieving a little less stressful. You have taken the time to show them even more how much they mean to you. Once you are gone, your gift-giving is over. What is the last gift you want them to remember you by? This is it. You have done it. You left them a gift of completion and being a good steward with your end-of-life. You also set an example for them on what they can do to leave the last gift for their loved ones. You can purchase this book and give it to them. They will appreciate the fact that you made your departure easier for them and you want them to do the same.

Now that you see how valuable this book is, encourage others in your family to follow your lead and get their end-of-life affairs in order. Tell them to order their book and continue the legacy for your family.

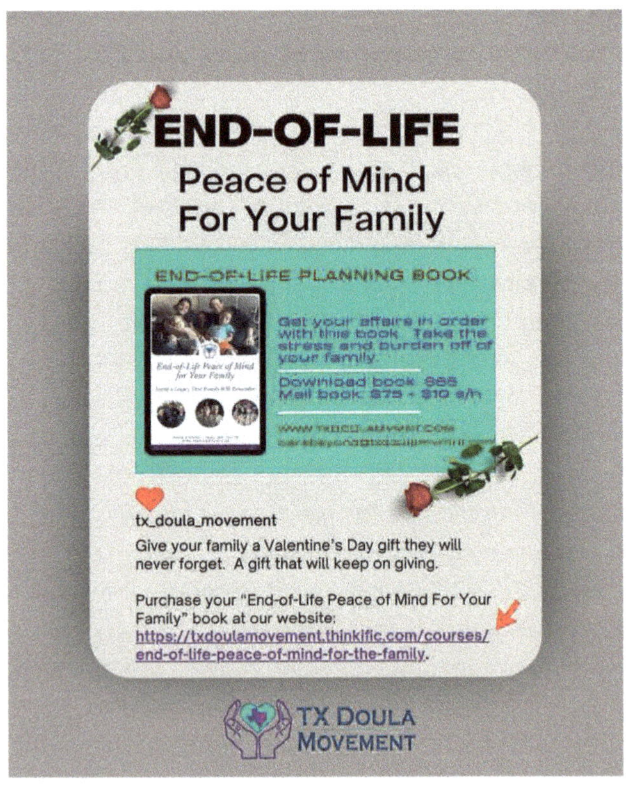

PROGRAMS
WE OFFER

We want you to be informed.

Many more services and
programs are listed
than what is here.

Thank You!

I hope this workbook has helped you plan for your End-of-Life. If you have any questions, please do not hesitate to contact us.

TX Doula Movement Team

Sonja Koenig, CEO & Founder
Emma Jane Frazier, Education Director

@TXDOULAMOVEMENT

WWW.TXDOULAMVMNT.COM

DOULASUPPORT@TXDOULAMVMNT.COM
CAREBEYOND@TXDOULAMVMNT.COM